Bringing Grandma Home

A Coronavirus Tale

Copyright 2020

ISBN- 978-1-7356245-2-5

All rights reserved.
No part of this publication may be reproduced, stored, distributed, or transmitted in any form or by any means, including photocopying, recording, or other electronic or mechanical methods, without the prior written permission of the publisher, except in the case of brief quotations embodied in critical reviews and certain other non commercial uses permitted by copyright law.

Printed in the United States of America

Dedicated to all the hard-working families that make books like "Bringing Grandma Home" possible.

Proceeds from this book will go to the From Boys to Men Network
A 501(C) (3) Non-Profit Foundation
Stanley G. Buford, Executive Director
7061 West North Avenue
Suite 163
Oak Park, IL 60302
fromboystomen@gmail.com

In Loving Memory

To my mother, Juanita Buford-Puckett…the inspiration for this book: Mom, thank you for inspiring everything positive begun by your children while encouraging us with love to "always do your best!"

With Special Thanks to my Contributors

Shanicka N. Scarbrough, M. D.
Alan Wilson, M. D.
Rosemarie Gillen, Illustrator
Lisa Michaels, Content Editor
Rev. Dr. Mark A. Henton, Pastor/Advisor

Family

Glen Buford, Brother
Danny Buford, Brother
Jerry Buford, Brother
Janice Buford, Sister
Terrence L. Buford, Son (Tee)
Kathryn C. Buford PhD., Daughter (Kay)

Foreword

Bringing Grandma Home: A Coronavirus Tale

Question: Are you frustrated about the coronavirus pandemic?

So are Tee and his sister, Kay. There are so many new rules to follow: Washing your hands. Staying six feet apart. Wearing a face mask. Worst of all, they can't just play with their friends like before.

Then, grandma gets sick with coronavirus. And that's when they learn the value of all those rules. They are there to keep us safe!

Join this journey of the heart as the family goes through Grandma's bout with the virus, and the wisdom that grandma uses to guide everyone; including a concerned mom and dad. She imparts the practical information on how to fight the virus, helping to protect her family and yours. It will be the slice of pie everyone needs during these crazy, pandemic times.

This book is a great tool for introducing children to the reasons for rules to fight the coronavirus. Recommended for grades kindergarten to eighth grade, it can be a catalyst for discussions at home or in the classroom. Filled with examples and practical applications, you'll have what you need to help introduce children to the necessities of the new societal rules and norms designed to defeat the coronavirus. As a Medical Doctor I have enjoyed reading this wonderful children's book and I am sure you will too!

Shanicka N. Scarbrough, M. D.

Bringing Grandma Home

A Coronavirus Tale

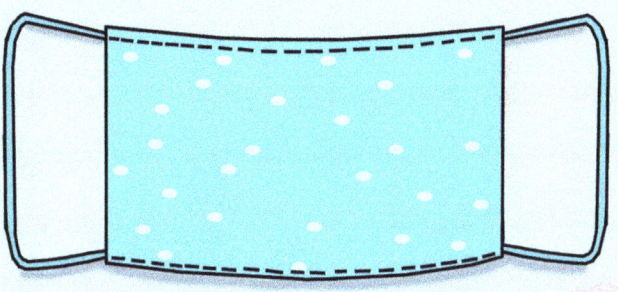

Written By Stanley G. Buford

Illustrated By Rosemarie Gillen

Foreword By
Shanicka N. Scarbrough M. D.

"It's been so LONG since they closed our school!"
Tee complained, "I'm bored silly!"

"I'm sorry you're stuck at home," Mom replied, "but you know why."

Tee and Kay rolled their eyes and chorused,
"Coronavirus!"

"Why can't we go to the park?" asked Tee, "I miss my friends!"

"I wish we could take a special trip somewhere,"
said Dad, "but I have to keep you safe."

"I'm feeling fidgety," said Kay.

"I've got ants in my pants!" Tee giggled.

"I'm tired of wearing a mask every time we go out," Tee complained.

Kay batted her eyelashes and said, "Mine matches my dress!"

Mom groaned, "My fingers are sore from all the soapy hand-washing."

"Mine too," Dad nodded, "but we have to if we want to eat or drink anything!"

Buzz-buzz……buzz-buzz….

Dad's phone vibrated next to the puzzle.

"Hello?" Dad answered. "She's where?"

When Dad finished the call, Mom asked, "Why do you look so worried?"

Exhaling, Dad explained, "Grandma has a fever. She's in the hospital with the Coronavirus, Covid 19."

"Oh no!" cried Kay.

"Will she be okay?" Tee questioned.

Tearfully, Dad replied, "I don't really know."

"I know what we'll do," Mom huddled them all together. "We'll pray for Grandma to get better, and when she does, we'll bring her home to stay with us."

"Can we go and visit Grandma?" asked Tee.

"I'll wash up and wear my mask!" Kay exclaimed.

"Visitors aren't allowed," said Dad, "and I'll bet you know why!"

Tee and Kay rolled their eyes and chorused,
"Coronavirus!"

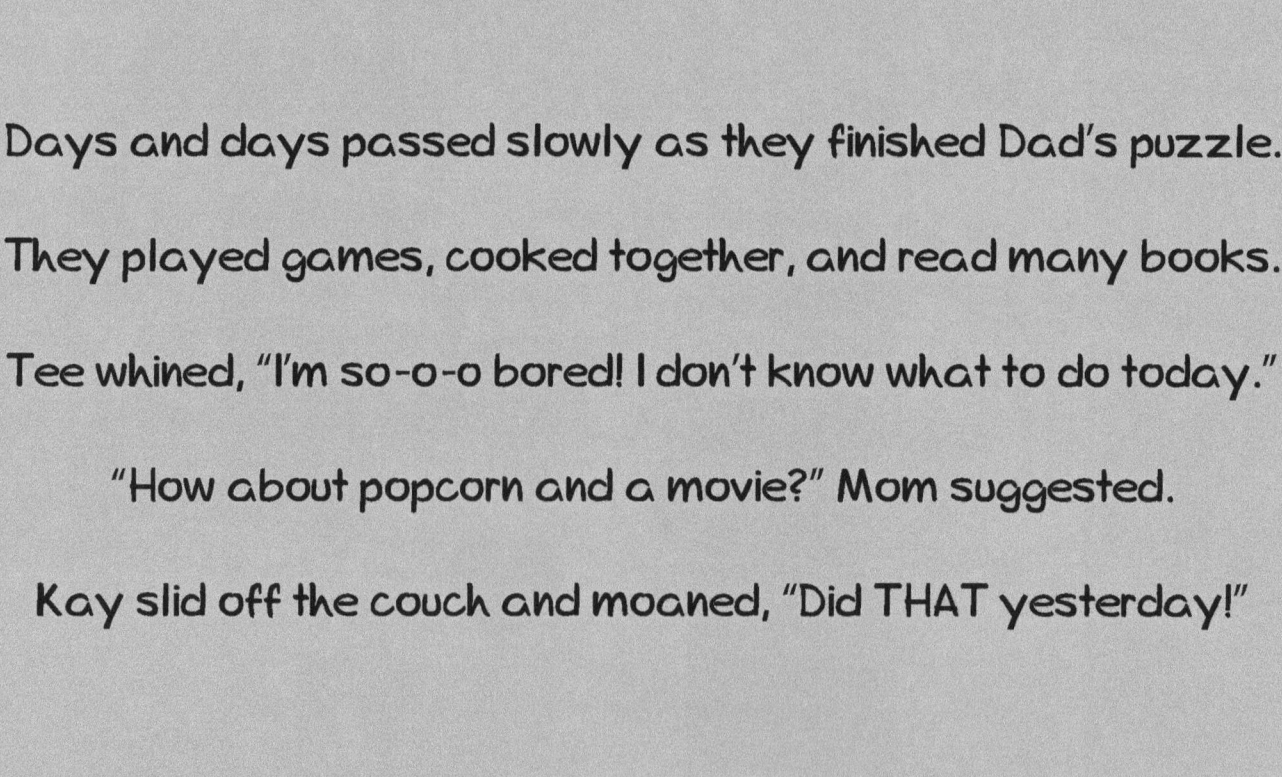

Days and days passed slowly as they finished Dad's puzzle.

They played games, cooked together, and read many books.

Tee whined, "I'm so-o-o bored! I don't know what to do today."

"How about popcorn and a movie?" Mom suggested.

Kay slid off the couch and moaned, "Did THAT yesterday!"

Dad peeked his head through the door and said,
"I've got a surprise for you!"

"GRANDMA!" they all shouted.

"Wait, wait, wait!" warned Dad, as the children bounced toward Grandma. "You can't hug her just yet."

"Hello Babies, give me a few minutes," Grandma smiled, "then we'll hug 'til the sunsets!"

Mom explained, "Grandma needs to wash off any germs she might have picked up in the hospital."

"We're just so happy you feel better," said Tee.

"And you're finally here!" Kay clapped with excitement.

After Grandma cleaned up she cuddled on the couch with her grandchildren. "Mom and Dad MADE us stay home forever!" complained Tee.

Kay added, "Grandma, we have to wash our hands way too much!"

Grandma giggled. "Everything they've done," she said, "they did to keep you safe from the very thing that made me sick. Do you know what it was?"

Tee and Kay chorused, "Coronavirus!"

"That's right!" said Grandma. "If you go out and play, you could get infected."

Mom said, "Some people have it and don't even know it!"

Dad chimed in, "Kids are getting it too. We don't want you to get sick like Grandma and so many others."

""My neighbor accidentally gave it to me," said Grandma, "so I want you to stay home and stay healthy!"

"Now I understand why we can't play with friends," said Tee.

"Me too," Kay agreed.

"We're glad you're okay Grandma. I'm going to go wash my hands now!"

The whole family was happy to finally be together.

"Staying home isn't so bad." said Tee, "as long as we have each other."

"Thank goodness we're all healthy," said Dad, squeezing Kay.

Mom nodded, "Yes, and we're going to do our best to keep it that way!"

Grandma chimed in with delight:

"Now who wants a slice of my fresh baked sweet potato pie?"

Tee, Kay, Mom and Dad all chorused...Meeee!

Grandmas Secret Recipe: Old Fashioned Sweet Potato Pie
(You must promise to never share this recipe with anyone besides mom and dad)

Ingredients

- 2 medium sized sweet potatoes (about 1-1/2 pounds), peeled and cubed
- 1/3 cup of butter (soften it up)
- 1/2 cup of sugar
- 2 large eggs (make sure you ask the chicken nicely) at room temperature, lightly beaten
- 3/4 cup of evaporated milk
- 1 teaspoon of real vanilla extract (imitation vanilla won't do)
- 1/2 teaspoon of ground cinnamon
- 1/2 teaspoon of ground nutmeg
- 1/4 teaspoon of rock salt
- 1 unbaked pie shell (9 inches)
- 1 squeeze of lemon peel

Directions

- Place sweet potatoes in a medium saucepan; add water to cover. Bring to a boil. Reduce heat; cook, uncovered, until tender (13-15 minutes). Drain potatoes; return to pan. Mash until very smooth; cool to room temperature.
- In a bowl, cream butter and sugar. Add eggs; mix well. Add milk, two cups of mashed sweet potatoes, vanilla, cinnamon, nutmeg, and salt; mix well. Pour into pie shell. Bake at 425° for 15 minutes. Reduce heat to 350°; bake until set or a knife inserted in the center comes out clean, about 35-40 minutes longer. Cool. Store in refrigerator.
- If you put pie out on window seal to cool, make sure there are no bears from the wild to steal it!

Note* This recipe must be finished under the watchful eye of an adult.

Bringing Grandma Home:
A Coronavirus Tale

By Stanley G. Buford

"We want more time off from school!" Says Tee and Kay.
But not how the unexpected vacation came their way.
It is scary to think about COVID-19,
Spending every day trying to stay clean.

Tee and Kay cannot go outside to play.
Their friends must also be at home to stay.
No parks, no shopping, and no special trips.
They can't go to the store to get some chips.

Tee and Kay are restless, like how trees in the wind sway.
"Mom and Dad!" they say. "Why can't we go out and play?"
"The weather is nice now, and I'll be really good!"
But, Mom and Dad would rather have them stay in their neighborhood.

It is tiring to remember to wash your hands every two hours.
Masks don't seem like they have superpowers.
"Wash your hands," Mom says, "and use some soap!"
It feels like the world has lost all of its hope.

The phone call rang in the morning quite loud.
Dad's face turned into a very dark cloud.
Grandma was in the hospital with COVID-19,
Even though she did her best to keep everything clean.

Tee and Kay tried to visit, but they wouldn't let them inside.
They sat outside the hospital, tears falling as they cried.
"Let's pray for Grandma," Dad said, "she'll be okay soon."
"Then you'll see her dance again to a cheery tune."

Two weeks later, Grandma finally got better.
She came home from the hospital in her favorite sweater.
Kay said, "This is the best thing that has happened today!"
"It has been months since there was anything good we could say!"

Tee and Kay want to hug Grandma, but they cannot just yet.
A warm bath and a change of clothes is the safest bet.
COVID-19 could linger on this or on that.
It's better to be safe than sorry with a virus you can't quite look at.

Grandma staying for a while feels like a decision hallowed,
But Tee and Kay don't like the rules that need to get followed.
Grandma said, "Your parents just want us all to be safe, my dears."
"You two getting sick is one of their greatest fears."

"There are many children and people now who are at risk."
"I got sick from a neighbor because we shared a bisque."
"Staying at home isn't always fun, but it helps you stay well."
"That way, you can avoid staying at the hospital for a spell."

Tee and Kay felt better after what Grandma said.
Although it would be nice if COVID-19 disappeared instead!
They understood more about why rules are so strict,
Especially since the virus is hard to predict.

Life gets better with everyone there at home.
Laughter echoes loudly as it finds hallways to roam.
The best part of the story, Tee and Kay cannot lie,
Is that Grandma is going to the kitchen to make her world-famous sweet potato pie!

COVID-19 Stay Safe Rules for Parents and Children

To avoid coming into contact with COVID-19, it is always a good practice to:

- Wash your hands regularly with soap and water for at least 20 seconds. About the time it takes to sing one verse of "Old McDonald Had a Farm."
- When running water is not available, use an alcohol-based hand rub (Hand Sanitizer), with at least 60% alcohol.
- Always wash clearly dirty hands.
- Avoid touching your eyes, nose, or mouth with unwashed hands.
- Practice good breathing, including covering your mouth when coughing or sneezing. Sneeze or cough into your elbow to avoid contact with mouth and hands.
- Avoid close contact with people who are sick (Grandma included).
- Practice Social Distancing: Try to stay about 6 feet away from people waiting in line for just about any purpose such as; store, lunch counter, or post office for example.
- Tell mom or dad if you think you're running a fever.
- Be kind to those that are not feeling well… Encourage them!
- Stay home if you are sick.

Author Bio

Stanley G. Buford was born in Chicago, Illinois. He studied at Illinois State University and holds master's degrees from National-Louis University in Management/Human Resource Development and DePaul University in Curriculum Development. He has worked as a "results-driven" teacher in Chicago Public Schools, the Archdioceses of Chicago and as a Learn Charter School Employee.

Stanley has appeared as a guest on the nationally televised show Heartbeat of America in a frank discussion concerning the challenges of climbing corporate and educational ladders. He owns and operates a state certified management consulting business, Terkat Consultants, Inc. He has been quoted in news articles while lecturing at schools such as Northwestern, DePaul and the University of Illinois on a variety of contemporary issues. An avid marathoner, actor, playwright and visionary, Stanley has served as the Program Director of the School Partnerships Program, a school improvement project at DePaul University. He has also served as an adjunct faculty member at Concordia University. He is a member of Monument of Faith Evangelistic Church, in Chicago, where he serves as President of the Men's Department and functions as Dean of Leadership and Christian Education Sector of the Richard Daniel Henton University. In 1995, he founded his mentoring program, From Boys To Men Network Foundation, to improve the quality of life for school-age boys in Chicago's inner city. He also directs all proceeds from the sale of his books to this nonprofit 501 (c) 3 program.

In this timely children's book, ***Bringing Grandma Home: A Coronavirus Tale***, Buford weaves the tale of two kids that finally realize mom and dad aren't just being strict with new rules because of the coronavirus outbreak. Grandma sets the record straight, having dealt with a bout of the ailment and survived. This new work is another rendition of success from a stellar 20-plus year teaching career in public, parochial and charter schools in Urban America. Bringing Grandma Home lives up to expectations characteristic of Buford's Award-winning writing style with drama, facts, humor and a dose of reality in the era of our New Normal.

This work is a follow-up to his Amazon.com bestseller: Not All Teachers Are Parents, But All Parents Are Teachers, endorsed by former President Barack Obama as: "An interesting book on parenting!"

www.ingramcontent.com/pod-product-compliance
Lightning Source LLC
Chambersburg PA
CBHW051302110526
44589CB00025B/2918